Ice Veil Tales

Coach's Playbook

Ora Munter

Coach's Playbook

The Guide Book for

Ice Veil Tales

Illustrated Book

Story/Coloring Book

E-Book

Audio Book

© Copyright 2017 Ora Munter

ISBN-13: 978-1979707985

ISBN-10: 1979707987

All rights reserved. No part of this publication may be reproduced, stored in a retrieval system, or transmitted, in any form or by any means, electronic, mechanical, photocopying, recording, or otherwise, without the written prior permission of the author.

CONTENTS

Introduction:
- Note to the Coach 4
- Script Starts Here 5
- How to Feel Inner Peace 6
- Bullies are Ignorant 7
- Your Secret Weapon 8

Book I: Cocovanilla and the Ice Veil 9

Book II: Chocolitz Invasion 15

Book III: Imagination Pad 18

Book IV: Space Pirates 20

Book V: Birds of Paradise 22

Book VI: Tootonzola Monster 24

Book VII: Reunion 26

Book VIII: Curse of the Golden Palace 30

Book IX: Lost Spirit 32

Book X: Shnorgorfs Visit 35

Book XI: Queen's Birthday 37

BLOOM Diary 41

Activities 56

INTRODUCTION
Note to the Coach

ICE VEIL TALES entertain kids while you and **COACH'S PLAYBOOK** teach them how to cope with their emotional reactions to bullies outside as well as inside their heads.

Please be prepared to focus your attention on your child.

Set aside quiet time in a safe space where you can comfortably interact.

COACH'S PLAYBOOK is an easy-to-follow script.

Your role is "C" as in Coach. Your child's role is "A" as in answer.

This is not a test. All answers are included so it is a no-brainer.

Comments, questions and answers are designed to enhance listening comprehension and heart-to-heart communication with your child.

If any emotional issues arise, ask your child to practice the belly breathing technique, "How to Feel Inner Peace" on page 6.

Trust her to find her answers within, and she will learn to trust herself.

ENJOY!

SCRIPT STARTS HERE

C: Let's talk about what you need to know about **YOU!**

First of all, did you know…?

You are a Miracle!

It is true!

It took Nature billions of years and millions of creatures before it figured out how to make human beings that could survive on planet earth.

Not only are you a miracle, you are also lucky to have been born into a group of humans called, Homo-sapiens.

Homo means man. Sapiens means wise.

The wisest thing you need to know is…

You are Alive!
Life is a Precious Gift.
You are Here to Enjoy.
For the Ultimate Joy You Need
INNER PEACE!

You need inner peace just as much as you need food, shelter and clothing.

Inner Peace is FREE! It has been inside you ever since you were born.

You may feel it any time, all the time, anywhere and everywhere.

Would you like to learn how to feel inner peace?

A: Yes.

How to Feel Inner Peace

1. **Close your mouth.** Breathe through your nose, because your nose hairs trap germs, keeping you healthy.

2. **Inhale.** The cool breeze that flows through your nose is the **Ice Veil**. Listen to its sound.

3. **Ride the Ice Veil's Peace Trail** down to your belly, up through your ribs, around your chest and…

4. **Exhale.** No one knows how the **Ice Veil** comes or where it goes. Yet it keeps you alive! Be grateful.

PRACTICE INHALE. EXHALE. TRUST THE ICE VEIL.

C: How does inner peace feel?
A: Like nothing.
C: By "nothing" do you mean you feel relaxed? Calm? Quiet?
A: Yes.
C: You are feeling it! Every moment you feel inner peace life gets better.

Now let's talk about **BULLIES**

Bullies are Ignorant. They Ignore Inner Peace.

You need inner peace to enjoy life.

Without inner peace we become mean and miserable bullies.

Miserable bullies only feel good when they are making others miserable.

You never know when a bully will strike because they never warn you.

Their favorite trick is a **SURPRISE ATTACK**.

That way you become confused, frightened, sad and mad.

Before you know it, they have stolen your inner peace.

What are some things bullies say or do to steal your inner peace?

A: They say I am stupid, ugly, etc.

C: **Just as bullies can attack you outside, they can also attack you inside your head.**

What are some thing bullies say inside your head?

A: I am stupid and ugly etc.

C: They say the same things inside your head as they say outside. That is because you recorded what they said and then replayed it inside your head.

Since you need inner peace to enjoy life, you have a **Secret Weapon** to help you hold onto that feeling.

Let's discover more about your **Secret Weapon.**

Your Secret Weapon is the Power of Choice.

When a Big Bully Attacks You Have **3** Choices.

1. BULLY YOURSELF

Listen to Bullies Inside Your Head.

When you record what the big bully said and then replay it inside your head over and over again, you make yourself miserable. You feel sorry for yourself for hours, even days. It is a sad waste of time. No fun for anyone.

2. BE A BULLY

Get Mad. Then Do Something Bad to Someone Else.

Without inner peace you will bully someone smaller to feel better. Then that person will get mad and bully someone smaller. Then that person will get mad and bully someone even smaller. And so on and so on. No fun for anyone.

3. BLOOM with PEACE

Inhale. Exhale. Trust the Ice Veil.

Riding the Ice Veil's Peace Trail calms you down, so you can think clearly and do what is right. Peace inside brings peace outside. Fun for everyone!

If Someone Bullies You, Do Not Bully Yourself or Others. Choose Inner Peace and Save Yourself a Lifetime of Misery.

✳ ✳ ✳

Let's begin **ICE VEIL TALES** and see how your Secret Weapon works.

"COCOVANILLA AND THE ICE VEIL" BOOK I

C: **ICE VEIL TALES** are about a little girl who learns how to outsmart big bullies. Let's learn along with her so you can outsmart bullies too.

SHOW BOOK I COVER:

The first story is, "Cocovanilla and the Ice Veil, Book I."

PRACTICE INHALE. EXHALE. TRUST THE ICE VEIL.

(Show Episode One of the Puppet Show: www.IceVeilTales.com.

Or read Chapter One. Then ask the following questions).

EPISODE ONE

C: Who was the bully and why?

A: Kiki bullied herself inside her own head.

C: Telling yourself nobody loves you is a nasty lie. Every breath you take is a priceless gift of pure love. Even the richest person in the world cannot buy a single breath.

Fill Yourself With Love and Let It Be Your Armor Against Bullies.

How did Cocovanilla save Kiki from drowning in sadness?

A: She showed her how to Ride the Ice Veil's Peace Trail.

C: What does this line mean? "Cocovanilla and Kiki merged."

A: Once you know how to feel inner peace, you know it forever.

C: What happened when Kiki rode the Ice Veil's Peace Trail?

A: She enjoyed the garden and flowers. She felt good.

C: When you feel inner peace, you are here now. The past no longer exists. Being here right now is called, the present. **You are Alive!!!**

Did the bully go away?

A: No. It was still inside her head. It told Cocovanilla to run away.

C: Did inner peace go away?

A: No. A soft voice called her name.

C: In every moment of your life you have a choice.

Either listen to the bully or to the Ice Veil. You can only listen to one. Let's see which one Cocovanilla listens to next.

PRACTICE INHALE. EXHALE. TRUST THE ICE VEIL. (Play Episode 2).

EPISODE TWO

C: Who was the biggest bully in Ice Dreamland and why?

A: The King of Kones. He polluted the air, imprisoned people in the Popsicle Freezer and ordered the Queen of Sorbet to marry him.

C: What did he threaten to do if the Queen disobeyed him?

A: Release the Giant, who would destroy the planet.

C: The miserable King of Kones would rather destroy the whole planet than allow others to live in peace. What was the Queen's reply?

A: She said she needed the Ice Veil for the wedding ceremony.

C: When a bully attacks, stall for time so you can figure out a peaceful solution. What is the best way to begin solving any problem?

A: Inhale. Exhale. Trust the Ice Veil.

PRACTICE INHALE. EXHALE. TRUST THE ICE VEIL. (Play Episode 3).

EPISODE THREE

C: What must Cocovanilla do to save Ice Dreamland?

A: She must carry two baskets to the Ice Palace before the bell tolls three times.

C: We all carry two baskets inside. One basket is full of peaceful feelings. The other basket is filled with sad, bad and mad feelings. We always have a choice where we stick our noses.

In this episode, who was the bully and why?

A: Cocovanilla imagined bullies attacking her in the Black Cherry Forest.

C: When you Ride the Ice Veil's Peace Trail, bullies back off, especially the ones in your imagination, because they are not real.

PRACTICE INHALE. EXHALE. TRUST THE ICE VEIL. (Play Episode 4).

EPISODE FOUR

C: Jamoca warned Cocovanilla to, "Walk quickly, but softly. Smoothly not gawky. If anyone dare be silent of your affair. And beware of Rocky Road." How could she have paid attention to that warning?

A: Inhale. Exhale. Trust the Ice Veil

C: Cocovanilla was right to feel concerned about entering the forest. Before you begin any challenge Ride the Ice Veil's Peace Trail.

It helps you stay cool, calm and focused.

If Cocovanilla had chosen inner peace, she would not have been scared by a silly little goose. Nor would she have chased Rocky Road. She would have simply said, "Dude, mind your own business." Then moved on.

It is okay to forget. We all do. Getting back on track is what it is all about. You never fail when you Ride the Ice Veil's Peace Trail.

Let's see what happens next.

PRACTICE INHALE. EXHALE. TRUST THE ICE VEIL. (Play Episode 5).

EPISODE FIVE

C: Who was the bully and why?

A: Rum Raisin was the bully because he plotted to destroy the Ice Veil.

C: The King of Kones bullied Rum Raisin. Then Rum Raisin got mad and did something bad. When bullies win peace loses!

We all need inner peace NOW. How do you re-connect with the present?

A: Inhale. Exhale. Trust the Ice Veil.

C: Always trust the Ice Veil. Things work out for the best when you do.

PRACTICE INHALE. EXHALE. TRUST THE ICE VEIL. (Play Episode 6).

EPISODE SIX

C: Who was the bully and why?

A: Crunch the troll, because he would not let Cocovanilla cross the bridge.

C: Cocovanilla listened to the Ice Veil.

Then she kindly listened to Crunch.

Listening to another person is like giving someone a piece of heaven.

She also kindly included him by inviting him to the wedding.

Kindness Connects Hearts. Bullies Break Hearts.

PRACTICE INHALE. EXHALE. TRUST THE ICE VEIL. (Play Episode 7).

EPISODE SEVEN

C: Pistachio did bad things because he believed the King would pay him.

But the bully King was lying and had no intention of keeping his promise.

Bullies are cruel and treat you like a fool.

They lie, cheat and steal to get what they want.

Without a lie detector, it is hard to know who is honest and who is not.

So when someone makes you a promise, write it down.

Honest people have no problem writing agreements.

Bullies never write agreements because without proof bullies lie.

They say they never made you a promise.

PRACTICE INHALE. EXHALE. TRUST THE ICE VEIL. (Play Episode 8).

EPISODE EIGHT

C: When Crunch played his tofutti trumpet the notes turned into butterflies. What does that say about Crunch?

A: Even though he looked like a troll outside, he had magic inside.

C: No matter what people look like outside, everyone has magic inside.

When the bell tolled Cocovanilla woke up and became jumpy.

In her rush she left behind the Ice Veil, the most important basket.

When you wake up in the morning or from a nap, inhale, exhale and trust the Ice Veil.

Feeling inner peace is the best way to start or refresh your day.

If Cocovanilla had done so, she would have remembered that she only needed two baskets, one with a red ribbon and one without.

Even in the worst of times, people can feel inner peace and work together to make peace happen outside.

Let's watch and see how.

PRACTICE INHALE. EXHALE. TRUST THE ICE VEIL.

(Play Episodes 9-12).

Chocolitz Invasion Book II

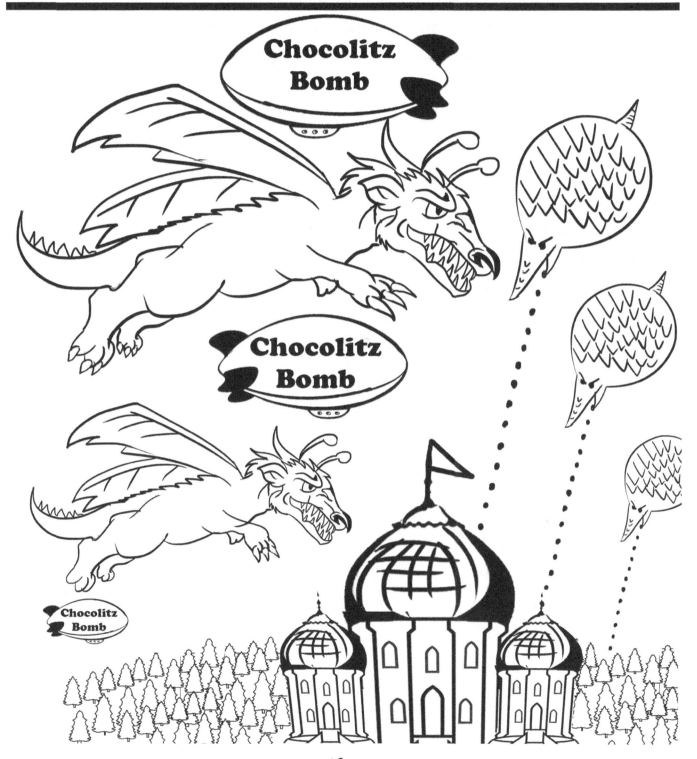

"CHOCOLITZ INVASION" BOOK II

CHAPTER ONE

SHOW BOOK II COVER:

C: Book Two is called, "Chocolitz Invasion."

These big, scary creatures are Chocolitz Nighthoppers.

These round guys are Rata-tatz. What are they doing?

A: Attacking Ice Dreamland.

PRACTICE INHALE. EXHALE. TRUST THE ICE VEIL.

READ CHAPTER ONE

C: We have just learned the King of Kones was in disguise. He was really the Emperor of the Planet of Dark Chocolitz and he wanted to stop Cocovanilla from fulfilling the Oracle of the Rising Peace Queens.

What did the Oracle say?

A: When 12 moons rise over Ice Dreamland, Peace Queens will rise up and bring happiness and prosperity to all.

C: Why did the Emperor want to stop Peace Queens from rising up?

A: He wanted everyone to be miserable.

C: Peace Queens have no time to waste on miserable bullies. Instead, they enjoy the magical gifts they were born to share.

PRACTICE INHALE. EXHALE. TRUST THE ICE VEIL.

CHAPTER TWO

READ CHAPTER TWO

C: Attacking people during a celebration is a cruel bully trick. Cocovanilla was kidnapped and Crunch is all alone. Let's hope they save themselves.

PRACTICE INHALE. EXHALE. TRUST THE ICE VEIL.

CHAPTER THREE

READ CHAPTER THREE

C: Crunch re-connected with his inner peace and then played his trumpet. His music reached those who cared about him.

When you feel lonely it is okay to ask for help. But first feel inner peace and then discover how peace happens outside.

PRACTICE INHALE. EXHALE. TRUST THE ICE VEIL.

CHAPTER FOUR

READ CHAPTER FOUR

C: What painful memory haunted Crunch?

A: He bullied his sister.

C: When we bully others, we dis-ease ourselves. Even if you pretend it never happened, your body remains dis-eased until you release those stressful feelings. Let's see how Crunch heals himself.

PRACTICE INHALE. EXHALE. TRUST THE ICE VEIL.

CHAPTER FIVE

READ CHAPTER FIVE

C: Crunch followed the Ice Veil's Peace Trail inside, and it guided him through the darkness outside. You can do the same thing whenever you feel lost. Let's see where it takes him.

PRACTICE INHALE. EXHALE. TRUST THE ICE VEIL.

CHAPTER SIX

READ CHAPTER SIX

C: What happened when Crunch apologized to his sister?

A: Light returned and Crunch transformed back into a Prince.

"IMAGINATION PAD" BOOK III

SHOW BOOK III COVER:

C: Book III is called, "Imagination Pad."

Humans are the only creatures on earth with an imagination.

Imagination helps us create ways to make our lives better.

Inner peace is the one thing you cannot create through your imagination.

Let's see what happens when you try.

PRACTICE INHALE. EXHALE. TRUST THE ICE VEIL.

(Read the entire story. Then discuss the following).

C: Who was the bully and why?

A: Balovalus was the ignorant bully because he ignored inner peace.

C: What did Balovalus do over and over again?

A: He imagined he could create inner peace by creating outer peace.

C: Every time he imagined peace, he created more and more misery.

Bullies refuse to accept inner peace and so they think they can imagine it.

Nobody can imagine inner peace.

The way peace works is, first you must feel it inside.

Then, like magic, you will experience peace outside.

The purpose of your imagination is to help you create things you want.

Know the difference between what you need and what you want.

You Cannot Imagine the Feeling You Need the Most, Inner Peace.

✳ ✳ ✳

SPACE PIRATES

BOOK IV

"SPACE PIRATES" BOOK IV

SHOW BOOK IV COVER:

C: Book IV is entitled, "Space Pirates."

In this story Crunch is the captain of a space ship and crew.

But Crunch forgets to practice inner peace.

Let's see what happens when you try to lead without inner peace.

PRACTICE INHALE. EXHALE. TRUST THE ICE VEIL.

(Read the entire story. Then discuss the following).

※ ※ ※

C: Crunch was lost in space.

He was confused and did not know what to do.

His crew went crazy and he ended up hiding underwater.

When he remembered to practice inner peace he found his answers.

He outsmarted the bullies and reclaimed his rocket ship.

He got back on track and did what he needed to do.

What will you do when you feel lost in confusion?

A: Inhale. Exhale. Trust the Ice Veil.

※ ※ ※

"BIRDS OF PARADISE" BOOK V

SHOW BOOK V COVER:

C: Book V "Birds of Paradise" is about birds and Slocum.

Notice the Slocum crawl. Let's see what helps them stand up.

PRACTICE INHALE. EXHALE. TRUST THE ICE VEIL.

(Read the entire story. Then discuss the following).

C: Which bird would you rather be?

The one who flies the skies and finds her own food?

Or the bird who wants her mama to feed her forever?

A: (Listen to their answers).

C: Why do you think Flabby Bird refused to take care of herself?

A: She was lazy and wanted to be babied.

C: She acted lazy. But the truth was, Flabby Bird was afraid she would fail.

Her fear kept her stuck on the tree branch.

First she became too fat to fly and feared she would fall.

Then she became so skinny the wind blew her out of the tree, and she feared she would become dinner.

Whenever You Feel Stuck in Fear, Choose Inner Peace Instead.

When you trust the Ice Veil, you will know how to take care of yourself and inspire others to stand up as well.

"TOOTONZOLA MONSTER" BOOK VI

SHOW BOOK VI COVER:

C: Book VI "Tootonzola Monster."

This story shows what it takes to overcome a really big bully.

PRACTICE INHALE. EXHALE. TRUST THE ICE VEIL.

(Read the whole story. Then discuss the following).

❋ ❋ ❋

C: Tootonzola Monster forced all the Bweeks to run and hide.

The best way to overcome evil is to do more good.

When Crunch agreed to help the Bweeks, he became practical-minded.

First, he observed Tootonzola and determined his strengths and weakness.

Second, Crunch checked out his resources. Resources are the tools and people power available to you.

Third, he came up with a clever plan.

Finally, he collaborated with the Bweeks. Collaboration means working with others. Together they put the plan into action and won!

When Crunch went through the dark tunnel, he trusted the Ice Veil to guide him to their queen.

When you are going through dark times, trust the Ice Veil to guide you back to the light.

Understand that everyone needs inner peace.

Collaborate and Bring Peace to As Many People as You Can.

❋ ❋ ❋

"REUNION" BOOK VII

CHAPTER ONE

SHOW BOOK VII COVER:

C: Book VII "Reunion."

Another big bully trap is the "Fake Father Figure."

The role of a Real Father is to love, support and protect you.

The goal of a "Fake Father Figure" is to control you.

A Real Father shows you he cares.

A "Fake Father Figure" tells you he cares. But then he threatens to punish you unless you obey him.

You have a secret weapon to help you escape the "Fake Father Figure" bully trap.

Let's see if Cocovanilla remembers to make the right choice.

***PRACTICE* INHALE. EXHALE. TRUST THE ICE VEIL.**

READ CHAPTER ONE

C: Why did the Silver Lighthopper tell Cocovanilla she must go through the blackest of Black Holes alone?

A: You can only feel inner peace for yourself. No one else can do it for you.

C: Bully traps are like black holes.

They suck you in and waste your precious time.

You Are The Angel Who Can Save You.

Let's see if Cocovanilla remembers how to save herself.

***PRACTICE* INHALE. EXHALE. TRUST THE ICE VEIL.**

CHAPTER TWO

READ CHAPTER TWO

C: What shocking news did the Emperor of Dark Chocolitz tell Cocovanilla?

A: He is her father.

C: He offered to take care of her. What did he demand in return?

A: She had to dance for him every night.

C: When she disobeyed, he sent her to the House of Chip Witches in the Slave Zone. Why did he do that?

A: He was punishing her for disobeying him.

C: Bullies feel powerful when others obey them. When you rebel, they punish you until you beg for mercy.

PRACTICE INHALE. EXHALE. TRUST THE ICE VEIL.

CHAPTER THREE

READ CHAPTER THREE

C: Who were the bullies and why?

A: The Chip Witch Sisters were mean and bossy to Cocovanilla.

C: The Chip Witch Sisters ignored inner peace and bullied Cocovanilla to feel better about themselves.

On the Planet of Dark Chocolitz the #1 rule is everyone must be miserable. Parents bully their children and children bully each other. No one knows any better. Everyone is stuck in the blackest of Black Holes.

In the world where Peace Queens rule, every day everyone practices inner peace and experiences joy. Both worlds exist inside of you. Which world will you choose?

A: The world of Peace Queens.

C: Let's see if Cocovanilla fulfills the Oracle of Rising Peace Queens.

PRACTICE INHALE. EXHALE. TRUST THE ICE VEIL.

CHAPTER FOUR

READ CHAPTER FOUR

C: Why did the Chip Witch Sisters want to marry Crunch?

A: They imagined he would save them from their misery.

C: When Crunch said he would "marry the one who is half vanilla," the Chip

Witch sisters almost destroyed themselves trying to please him.

Never harm yourself to please others. Anyone who asks you to harm yourself does not care about you.

PRACTICE INHALE. EXHALE. TRUST THE ICE VEIL.

CHAPTER FIVE

READ CHAPTER FIVE

C: What did Crunch say when he saw Cocovanilla?

A: He called her "the bitterest chocolitz of all."

C: When Crunch and Cocovanilla met at the bridge, Cocovanilla did not judge his looks. Instead she was kind and brought out his goodness.

How can you see the good in others?

A: First see the good in yourself. Inhale. Exhale. Trust the Ice Veil.

C: When you see the bad in others you bring out the bad in yourself. And so Crunch turned back into a troll.

In our imaginations we expect a Big Daddy or a Prince will give us everything we want and then we will be happy and feel loved.

Expectations Are Bully Traps For Disappointment.

When you practice inner peace, you have the strength to overcome all bullies and fill yourself with everything you need.

Trust the Ice Veil.

"CURSE OF THE GOLDEN PALACE" BOOK VIII

SHOW BOOK VIII COVER:

C: Book VIII is "Curse of the Golden Palace."

In this story Crunch is confident he can break the curse of the Golden Palace. After all, he broke Nanny Gorf's curse that turned him into a troll.

Let's see if he succeeds this time.

PRACTICE INHALE. EXHALE. TRUST THE ICE VEIL.

(Read the entire story. Then ask the following).

C: What did Crunch discover when he finally awakened?

A: Bullies can attack you even while you sleep.

Whenever you feel trapped in a nightmare, remember to inhale, exhale and trust the Ice Veil.

You will wake up and the nightmare will disappear without a trace.

LOST SPIRIT

BOOK IX

"LOST SPIRIT" BOOK IX

CHAPTER ONE

SHOW BOOK IX COVER:

C: Book IX is called "Lost Spirit."

This story is about Gorfina and Dr. Gorfitz, highly trained bullies. Let's see what traps they lay and tricks they play.

PRACTICE INHALE. EXHALE. TRUST THE ICE VEIL.

READ CHAPTER ONE

C: How did Gorfina steal Cocovanilla's happiness?

A: She concocted a polluted potion and Cocovanilla breathed in misery.

C: Pollution is nasty because we need air to live.

Let's see how Cocovanilla finds her happiness again.

PRACTICE INHALE. EXHALE. TRUST THE ICE VEIL.

CHAPTER TWO

READ CHAPTER TWO

C: Dr. Gorfitz lied by calling himself a "doctor."

He told Crunch to give Cocovanilla everything she wanted in order to feel happy again. What did she want?

A: Food and entertainment.

C: True joy only comes from feeling inner peace and gratitude for your precious gift of life.

Let's see if she remembers.

PRACTICE INHALE. EXHALE. TRUST THE ICE VEIL.

CHAPTER THREE

READ CHAPTER THREE

C: Dr. Gorfitz fell on his own knife. How was his death like the death of Madame Chip Witch?

A: They destroyed themselves with their own weapons.

C: When you use weapons you risk hurting yourself.

PRACTICE INHALE. EXHALE. TRUST THE ICE VEIL.

CHAPTER FOUR

READ CHAPTER FOUR

C: Gorfina brought the weapon and destroyed herself. What happened?

A: Crunch forced Gorfina to drink her evil potion. Then she vomited green slime, dove into the sea and drank herself to death.

C: Cocovanilla still needed to find her happiness. Let's find out how she found it.

PRACTICE INHALE. EXHALE. TRUST THE ICE VEIL.

CHAPTER FIVE

READ CHAPTER FIVE

C: What did the Silver Lighthopper say to Cocovanilla?

A: "I never left you. You left me. I am always here."

C: Forgetting the Ice Veil is a big bully trap. You can get lost in black holes of dark thoughts for days, years, even a lifetime.

Though Crunch helped as best as he could, it was finally up to Cocovanilla to save herself.

Inner Peace Never Leaves. It is Always Inside You.

It works like magic every time. Save yourself for the fun of it!

BOOK X

Shnorgorfs Visit

"SHNORGORFS VISIT" BOOK X

SHOW BOOK X COVER:

C: Book X "Shnorgorfs Visit." What do you see?

A: A happy Shnorgorf and an angry Shnorgorf.

C: We all have two sides, a peaceful and a bully side.

Let's see how we can bring out the best in ourselves.

PRACTICE INHALE. EXHALE. TRUST THE ICE VEIL.

(Read the entire story. Then discuss the following).

C: When a Shnorgorf stole the mango, Cocovanilla got mad and turned into a bully.

She chased, grabbed and shamed the Shnorgorf.

Then the Shnorgorf got mad and took revenge.

He and his buddies bullied Cocovanilla and Crunch out of their home.

When you live by these 3 rules you will save yourself a lot of misery.

   1. **Do not bully.**
   2. **Do not be bullied.**
   3. **But if you are bullied, do not take revenge.**

What could Cocovanilla have done instead of bullying the Shnorgorf?

A: She could have chosen to feel inner peace and let the Shnorgorf enjoy the mango.

C: She could have also helped the Shnorgorfs find dignified ways to take care of themselves.

"QUEEN'S BIRTHDAY" BOOK XI

CHAPTER ONE

SHOW BOOK XI COVER:

C: "Queen's Birthday" Book XI.

Birthdays are celebrations of life. But something is not right here.

Let's find out what went wrong.

PRACTICE Inhale. Exhale. Trust the Ice Veil.

READ CHAPTER ONE

C: Why did the Queen of Sorbet refuse to search for Gorfoon?

A: She wanted everyone to prepare for her birthday celebration.

C: Saving a life is more important than a party, no matter whose party or whose life it is. Do you agree?

A: Yes.

PRACTICE Inhale. Exhale. Trust the Ice Veil.

CHAPTER TWO

READ CHAPTER TWO

C: When no one listened to Butter Pecan, what did he do?

A: He told his problem to Pistachio.

C: When you have a problem it helps to talk with a friend.

But never tell an enemy your problems. Here is why.

PRACTICE Inhale. Exhale. Trust the Ice Veil.

CHAPTER THREE

READ CHAPTER THREE

C: The Queen of Sorbet refused to help the Cinnamon Gorfs find Gorfoon.

The Cinnamon Gorfs got mad and refused to help save Ice Dreamland.

What would have been a better solution?

A: King Egorf could have brought the Queen of Sorbet a birthday gift and respectfully asked her to reconsider her decision.

C: If someone bullies you, do not take revenge. Choose inner peace. Calm yourself. Think clearly. Then do what is right.

PRACTICE INHALE. EXHALE. TRUST THE ICE VEIL.

CHAPTER FOUR

READ CHAPTER FOUR

C: Why did Pistachio take the Queen of Sorbet's "happy spirit?"

A: He wanted revenge because the Queen snubbed him.

C: No one can take your "Happy Spirit." The Queen chose to bully herself with Pistachio's misery. Feeling guilty, however, does not bring back peace.

Let's find out how the Queen of Sorbet brings back peace and dignity to all.

PRACTICE INHALE. EXHALE. TRUST THE ICE VEIL.

CHAPTERS FIVE

READ CHAPTER FIVE

C: Though the war ended, there was no peace in Ice Dreamland. Cocovanilla and Crunch asked Gorfu what to do. What did he tell them?

A: "All of your answers are inside of you."

C: How did they find their answers?

A: They inhaled, exhaled and trusted the Ice Veil.

C: Gorfoon returned. But did the Cinnamon Gorfs forgive the Queen?

A: No.

C: More people in Ice Dreamland had to practice inner peace before there could be outer peace in Ice Dreamland.

The More People Practice Inner Peace, the More Peaceful the World Becomes.

PRACTICE INHALE. EXHALE. TRUST THE ICE VEIL.

CHAPTERS SIX & SEVEN

READ CHAPTERS SIX & SEVEN

C: When the Queen of Sorbet understood that everyone's life is precious and deserves kindness, the Ice Veil showered the planet with joy.

Here is your last question. If you were Kiki ice skating alone in the park and a snowstorm blew in, what would you do?

1. Bully Yourself. Feel sorry for yourself by listening to the bully recordings inside your head? Or…
2. Be a Peace Queen. Ride the Ice Veil's Peace Trail. Calm yourself, think clearly and then find shelter from the storm?

A: Be a Peace Queen.

In the beginning we talked about the recorder in your head.

Instead of recording bullies and replaying their tapes until you become miserable too, now you can start recording all your experiences as a Peace Queen.

BLOOM DIARY can help you bounce back to being a Peace Queen when bullies attack.

Let's see how it works.

PROPERTY OF _____

BLOOM DIARY

Bullies cause stress.

Stress feels like

you are being squeezed tight.

You need to **BLOOM** and feel inner peace **NOW!**

Here is how.

B

Breathe. When bullies attack hearts race and muscles brace. Release your stress. Slowly **Inhale. Exhale. Trust the Ice Veil.**

L

Listen to the Ice Veil as it flows through your nose.

O

Open up inside. Ride the Ice Veil's Peace Trail. Breathe down to your belly and up through your ribs and chest. Breathing in oxygen relaxes you.

O

Opportunities. Calm again, you can think clearly about your choices. Then choose the right thing to do.

M

Move forward with confidence knowing you are doing your best.

Own Your Secret Weapon!

Practice bouncing back from bully attacks

12 times with this diary.

Then choose to use it for the rest of your life.

BLOOM WITH PEACE!

BLOOM # _____   Date: _____

Dear Diary, when I woke up I **inhaled, exhaled,** and trusted the Ice Veil.
I said, "Thank you for today" and I felt… *(Choose and color your feelings)*.

Then along came a bully and I felt… *(Choose and color your feelings)*.

I needed to feel Peace again. So I practiced **BLOOM**.

- ❖ **B**reathe. **Inhale. Exhale. Trust the Ice Veil.**
- ❖ **L**isten to the Ice Veil flow through your nose.
- ❖ **O**pen up inside. Ride the Ice Veil through your belly, ribs, and chest.
- ❖ **O**pportunities. What are your choices? Choose the right one.
- ❖ **M**ove forward with confidence knowing you are doing your best.

How do you feel when you Bloom? *(Choose and color your feelings)*.

BLOOM # _____   Date: _____

Dear Diary, when I woke up I **inhaled, exhaled, and trusted the Ice Veil.**
I said, "Thank you for today" and I felt... *(Choose and color your feelings).*

Then along came a bully and I felt... *(Choose and color your feelings).*

I needed to feel Peace again. So I practiced **BLOOM**.

- **B**reathe. **Inhale. Exhale. Trust the Ice Veil.**
- **L**isten to the Ice Veil flow through your nose.
- **O**pen up inside. Ride the Ice Veil through your belly, ribs, and chest.
- **O**pportunities. What are your choices? Choose the right one.
- **M**ove forward with confidence knowing you are doing your best.

How do you feel when you Bloom? *(Choose and color your feelings).*

BLOOM # _____   Date: _____

Dear Diary, when I woke up I **inhaled, exhaled, and trusted the Ice Veil.**
I said, "Thank you for today" and I felt… *(Choose and color your feelings).*

Then along came a bully and I felt… *(Choose and color your feelings).*

I needed to feel Peace again. So I practiced **BLOOM**.

- ❖ **B**reathe. **Inhale. Exhale. Trust the Ice Veil.**
- ❖ **L**isten to the Ice Veil flow through your nose.
- ❖ **O**pen up inside. Ride the Ice Veil through your belly, ribs, and chest.
- ❖ **O**pportunities. What are your choices? Choose the right one.
- ❖ **M**ove forward with confidence knowing you are doing your best.

How do you feel when you Bloom? *(Choose and color your feelings).*

BLOOM # _____   Date: _____

Dear Diary, when I woke up I **inhaled, exhaled, and trusted the Ice Veil.**
I said, "Thank you for today" and I felt... *(Choose and color your feelings)*.

Then along came a bully and I felt... *(Choose and color your feelings)*.

I needed to feel Peace again. So I practiced **BLOOM**.

- ❖ **B**reathe. **Inhale. Exhale. Trust the Ice Veil.**
- ❖ **L**isten to the Ice Veil flow through your nose.
- ❖ **O**pen up inside. Ride the Ice Veil through your belly, ribs, and chest.
- ❖ **O**pportunities. What are your choices? Choose the right one.
- ❖ **M**ove forward with confidence knowing you are doing your best.

How do you feel when you Bloom? *(Choose and color your feelings)*.

BLOOM # _____   **Date:** _____

Dear Diary, when I woke up I **inhaled, exhaled, and trusted the Ice Veil.**
I said, "Thank you for today" and I felt… *(Choose and color your feelings)*.

Then along came a bully and I felt… *(Choose and color your feelings)*.

I needed to feel Peace again. So I practiced **BLOOM**.

- ❖ **B**reathe. **Inhale. Exhale. Trust the Ice Veil.**
- ❖ **L**isten to the Ice Veil flow through your nose.
- ❖ **O**pen up inside. Ride the Ice Veil through your belly, ribs, and chest.
- ❖ **O**pportunities. What are your choices? Choose the right one.
- ❖ **M**ove forward with confidence knowing you are doing your best.

How do you feel when you Bloom? *(Choose and color your feelings)*.

BLOOM # _____   Date: _____

Dear Diary, when I woke up I **inhaled, exhaled, and trusted the Ice Veil.**
I said, "Thank you for today" and I felt... *(Choose and color your feelings).*

Then along came a bully and I felt... *(Choose and color your feelings).*

I needed to feel Peace again. So I practiced **BLOOM**.

- ❖ **B**reathe. **Inhale. Exhale. Trust the Ice Veil.**
- ❖ **L**isten to the Ice Veil flow through your nose.
- ❖ **O**pen up inside. Ride the Ice Veil through your belly, ribs, and chest.
- ❖ **O**pportunities. What are your choices? Choose the right one.
- ❖ **M**ove forward with confidence knowing you are doing your best.

How do you feel when you Bloom? *(Choose and color your feelings).*

BLOOM #_____   Date: _____

Dear Diary, when I woke up I **inhaled, exhaled,** and trusted the Ice Veil. I said, "Thank you for today" and I felt... *(Choose and color your feelings).*

Then along came a bully and I felt... *(Choose and color your feelings).*

I needed to feel Peace again. So I practiced **BLOOM**.

❖ **B**reathe. **Inhale. Exhale. Trust the Ice Veil.**
❖ **L**isten to the Ice Veil flow through your nose.
❖ **O**pen up inside. Ride the Ice Veil through your belly, ribs, and chest.
❖ **O**pportunities. What are your choices? Choose the right one.
❖ **M**ove forward with confidence knowing you are doing your best.

How do you feel when you Bloom? *(Choose and color your feelings).*

BLOOM # _____   Date: _____

Dear Diary, when I woke up I **inhaled, exhaled, and trusted the Ice Veil.**
I said, "Thank you for today" and I felt... *(Choose and color your feelings).*

Then along came a bully and I felt... *(Choose and color your feelings).*

I needed to feel Peace again. So I practiced **BLOOM**.

❖ **B**reathe. **Inhale. Exhale. Trust the Ice Veil.**
❖ **L**isten to the Ice Veil flow through your nose.
❖ **O**pen up inside. Ride the Ice Veil through your belly, ribs, and chest.
❖ **O**pportunities. What are your choices? Choose the right one.
❖ **M**ove forward with confidence knowing you are doing your best.

How do you feel when you Bloom? *(Choose and color your feelings).*

BLOOM # _____   Date: _____

Dear Diary, when I woke up I **inhaled, exhaled, and trusted the Ice Veil.**
I said, "Thank you for today" and I felt... *(Choose and color your feelings)*.

Then along came a bully and I felt... *(Choose and color your feelings)*.

I needed to feel Peace again. So I practiced **BLOOM**.

- ❖ **B**reathe. **Inhale. Exhale. Trust the Ice Veil.**
- ❖ **L**isten to the Ice Veil flow through your nose.
- ❖ **O**pen up inside. Ride the Ice Veil through your belly, ribs, and chest.
- ❖ **O**pportunities. What are your choices? Choose the right one.
- ❖ **M**ove forward with confidence knowing you are doing your best.

How do you feel when you Bloom? *(Choose and color your feelings)*.

BLOOM # _____   **Date:** _____

Dear Diary, when I woke up I **inhaled, exhaled, and trusted the Ice Veil.**
I said, "Thank you for today" and I felt... *(Choose and color your feelings).*

Then along came a bully and I felt... *(Choose and color your feelings).*

I needed to feel Peace again. So I practiced **BLOOM.**

- **B**reathe. **Inhale. Exhale. Trust the Ice Veil.**
- **L**isten to the Ice Veil flow through your nose.
- **O**pen up inside. Ride the Ice Veil through your belly, ribs, and chest.
- **O**pportunities. What are your choices? Choose the right one.
- **M**ove forward with confidence knowing you are doing your best.

How do you feel when you Bloom? *(Choose and color your feelings).*

BLOOM # _____   Date: _____

Dear Diary, when I woke up I **inhaled, exhaled,** and trusted the Ice Veil.
I said, "Thank you for today" and I felt... *(Choose and color your feelings)*.

Then along came a bully and I felt... *(Choose and color your feelings)*.

I needed to feel Peace again. So I practiced **BLOOM**.

- ❖ **B**reathe. **Inhale. Exhale. Trust the Ice Veil.**
- ❖ **L**isten to the Ice Veil flow through your nose.
- ❖ **O**pen up inside. Ride the Ice Veil through your belly, ribs, and chest.
- ❖ **O**pportunities. What are your choices? Choose the right one.
- ❖ **M**ove forward with confidence knowing you are doing your best.

How do you feel when you Bloom? *(Choose and color your feelings)*.

BLOOM #_____   Date: _____

Dear Diary, when I woke up I **inhaled, exhaled, and trusted the Ice Veil.**
I said, "Thank you for today" and I felt... *(Choose and color your feelings)*.

Then along came a bully and I felt... *(Choose and color your feelings)*.

I needed to feel Peace again. So I practiced **BLOOM**.

- ❖ **B**reathe. **Inhale. Exhale. Trust the Ice Veil.**
- ❖ **L**isten to the Ice Veil flow through your nose.
- ❖ **O**pen up inside. Ride the Ice Veil through your belly, ribs, and chest.
- ❖ **O**pportunities. What are your choices? Choose the right one.
- ❖ **M**ove forward with confidence knowing you are doing your best.

How do you feel when you Bloom? *(Choose and color your feelings)*.

Activities

Mindful Coloring

Kids may color the Book Cover pictures while practicing inner peace.

Improvisation Exercise

Acting helps kids recognize and choose their feelings.

1. Ask kids which episode/chapter they enjoyed the most.
2. Take a vote. Once you have a winner, show or read that scene again.
3. Now ask for two volunteers to perform the scene.
4. Offer the volunteers a choice between two different colored capes. Costumes help kids express their feelings without inhibition.
5. Ask them to improvise the scene.
6. Now switch roles and capes. Ask the same two kids to play the opposite character. Playing both roles helps kids experience being the bully and the victim.
7. Discuss: How does it feel to be mean and make someone sad?

    How do you feel when a bully attacks?

    How do you feel when you use your Secret Weapon?

Collaborate

If your child sees bullying in her classroom…

1. Invite her classmates and parents to a meeting in your home.
2. Ask your child to lead the meeting.
3. She may begin by saying, "I have noticed that one classmate is bullying another. I will not name the bully or the victim."
4. Ask everyone to suggest what can be done to stop the bully.

BLOOM WITH PEACE!

The End

Made in the USA
Las Vegas, NV
24 April 2024

89080323R00033